AF326566

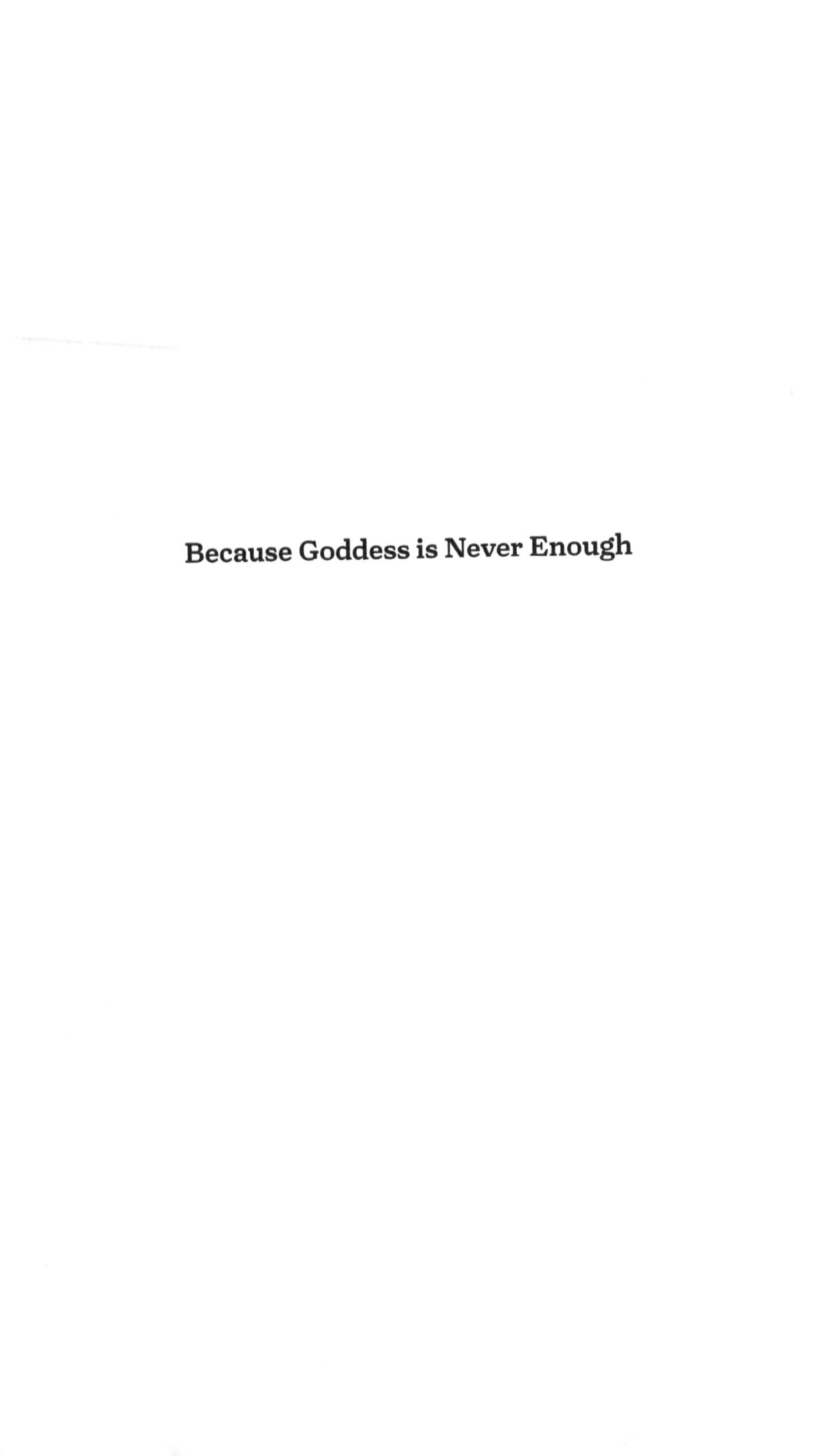

Because Goddess is Never Enough

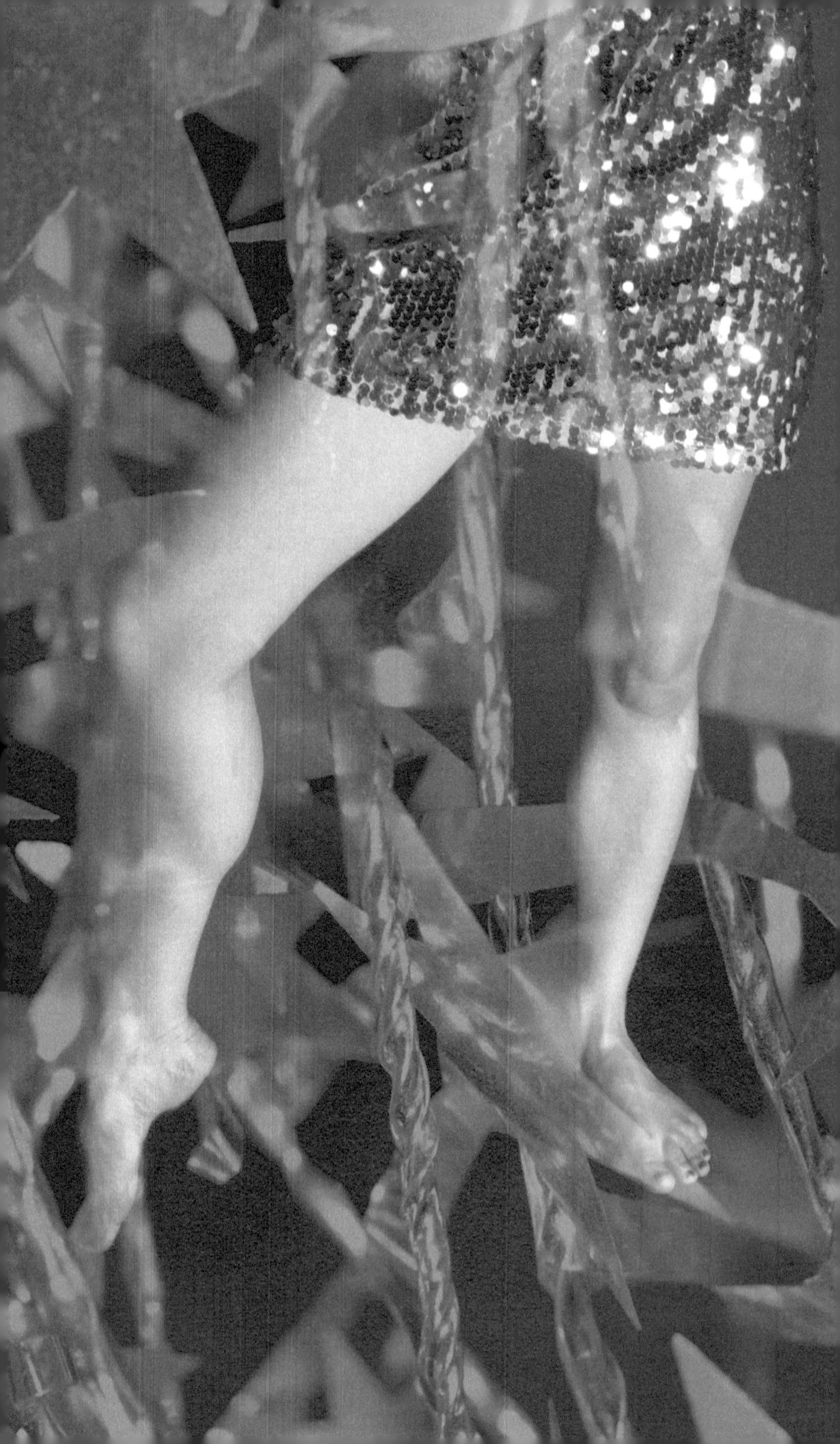

Because Goddess is Never Enough

*The book of the film**

Rosie Garland & Jane Glennie

*with bonus material

ISBN 978-1-912384-16-7

1st edition. First published 2022
by Peculiarity Press.

Design by Jane Glennie. Typeset in Turnip.

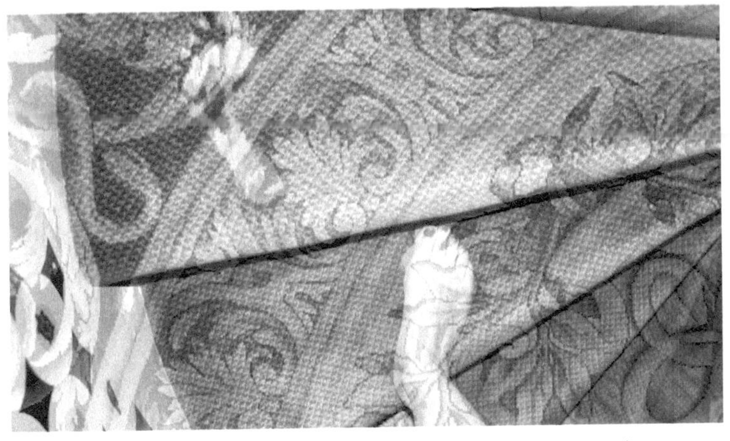

"Women have historically struggled to control their narratives...
they do not get to assert their position until they have 'paid their dues.'
To gain power – and crucially, to retain it – you need a reserve of it
to begin with."
Grace Medford, *The Guardian*, 19 February 2021

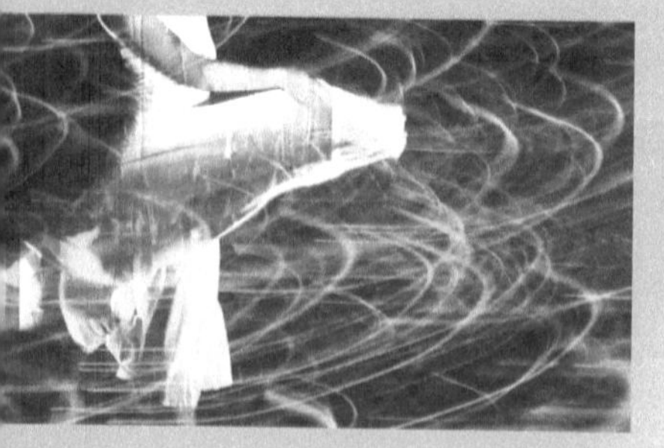

Who was Tilly Losch? Dancer, artist,
choreographer, lover, wife, muse …
Tilly seems a blur, glimpsed at the corner
of the eye, dancing in and out of focus.

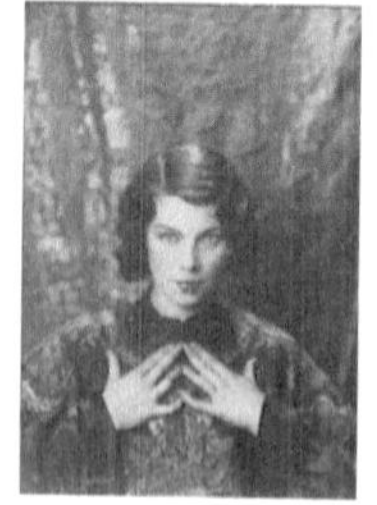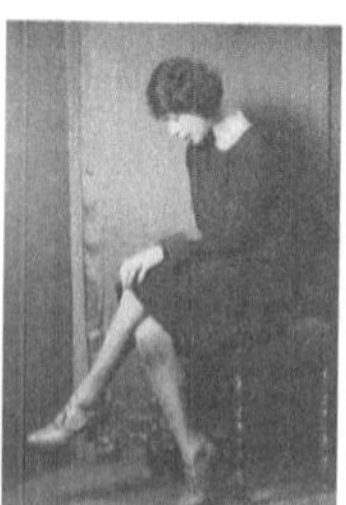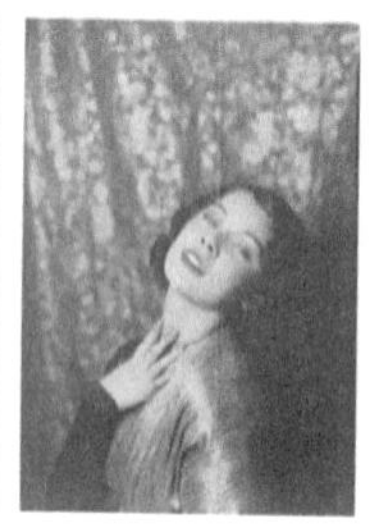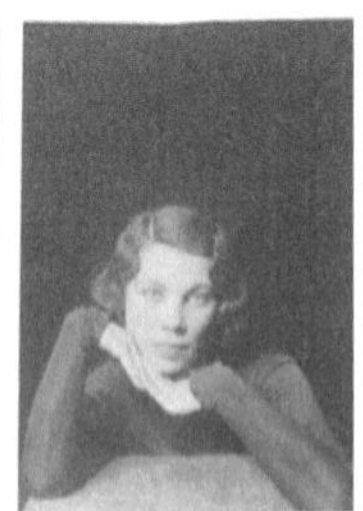

This book, and the film it grew out of, is a collaboration between filmmaker Jane Glennie and writer/performer Rosie Garland. They ask questions about biographies of women who fall into the footnotes, lost from history as so many women's stories are, and discover hope in reclaiming her-stories.

Tilly Losch was an Austrian dancer who lived and worked with prominent and cutting-edge choreographers and artists in the UK and the US, from the West End to Hollywood. She was also a choreographer in her own right, and later turned to painting.

Through images and poetry Glennie and Garland explore the elusive and fragmentary nature of Tilly's life, evoking the spirit of the 1920s–40s when she was at the peak of her fame.

'*Because Goddess is never enough*' is about self-worth and the credibility of creative women – Losch was someone who was at times exploited yet determined to maintain a path of her own making despite the obstacles that were very present in her era.

Glennie and Garland consider the complexity of female identity both then and now. Highlighting how far women have come in 90 years, and yet how far they still have to go to get recognition and true independence.

Because Goddess

is never enough

fallen into the footnotes [1,2,3,4,5,6,7,8,9]
slipped into the margins /
a numbered reference /
addenda /

[1] Edward James
[2] Cecil Beaton
[3] Fred Astaire
[4] Joseph Cornell
[5] Earl of Carnarvon

she dances in the index /
blink and you'll miss her /
Tilly /
Leopoldine /
piecing together a life from scraps /
enough of being pinned to wealthy velvet /
peeping through her own story /
off-kilter /
off the page /
away

[6] George Balanchine

[7] Orson Welles

[8] Randolph Churchill

[9] *Et al*

She's a tangle of celluloid
on the cutting-room floor. She is
minor interest. Not important enough
to be remembered. Not big enough
to be written out of history. Exists only
in reference to men. She is
wife, lover, dalliance, concubine.
She is 'seen in the company of —'
X with question mark.

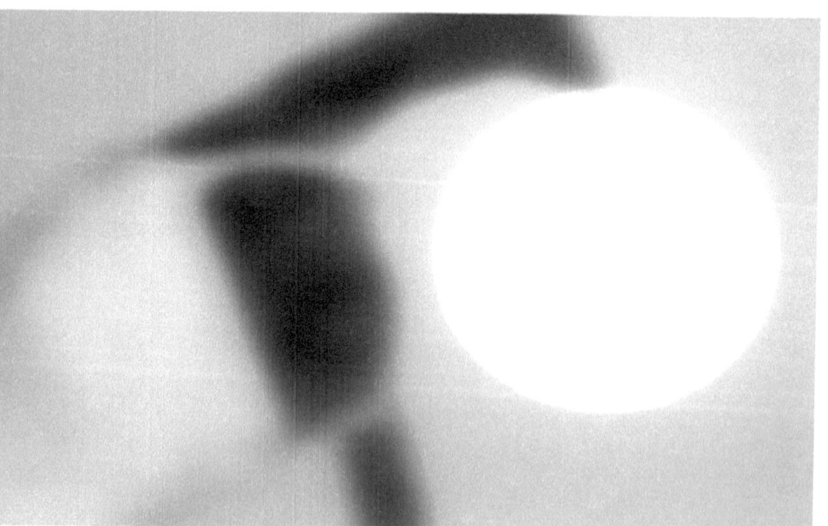

Where do I go
when I close
my eyes?

She is a blur. Only in focus
when her comet swings round
a bright man's sun and she is lit
by his importance. Never allowed
to be her own source of light.
Her radiance overlooked.
No value placed. Imagine
if she'd been born a man. She'd
be famous.

He is feted / she is omitted.

She will never run the risk of being rescued. She will never run the risk of escaping, however fast she runs. These men are hunters, walls hung with shotguns, swords, the stuffed heads of beasts and birds killed for the thrill of seeing them try to get away.

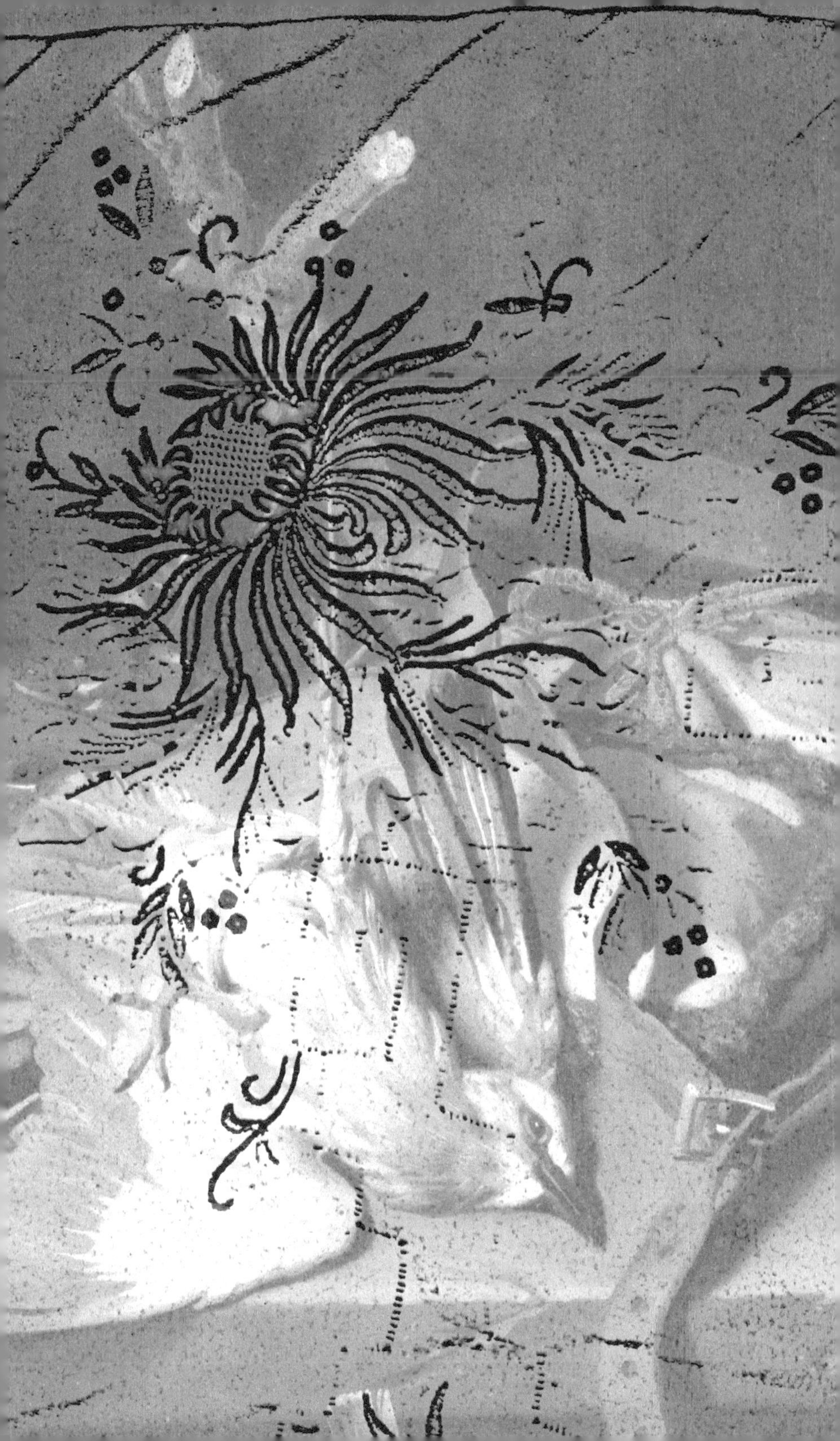

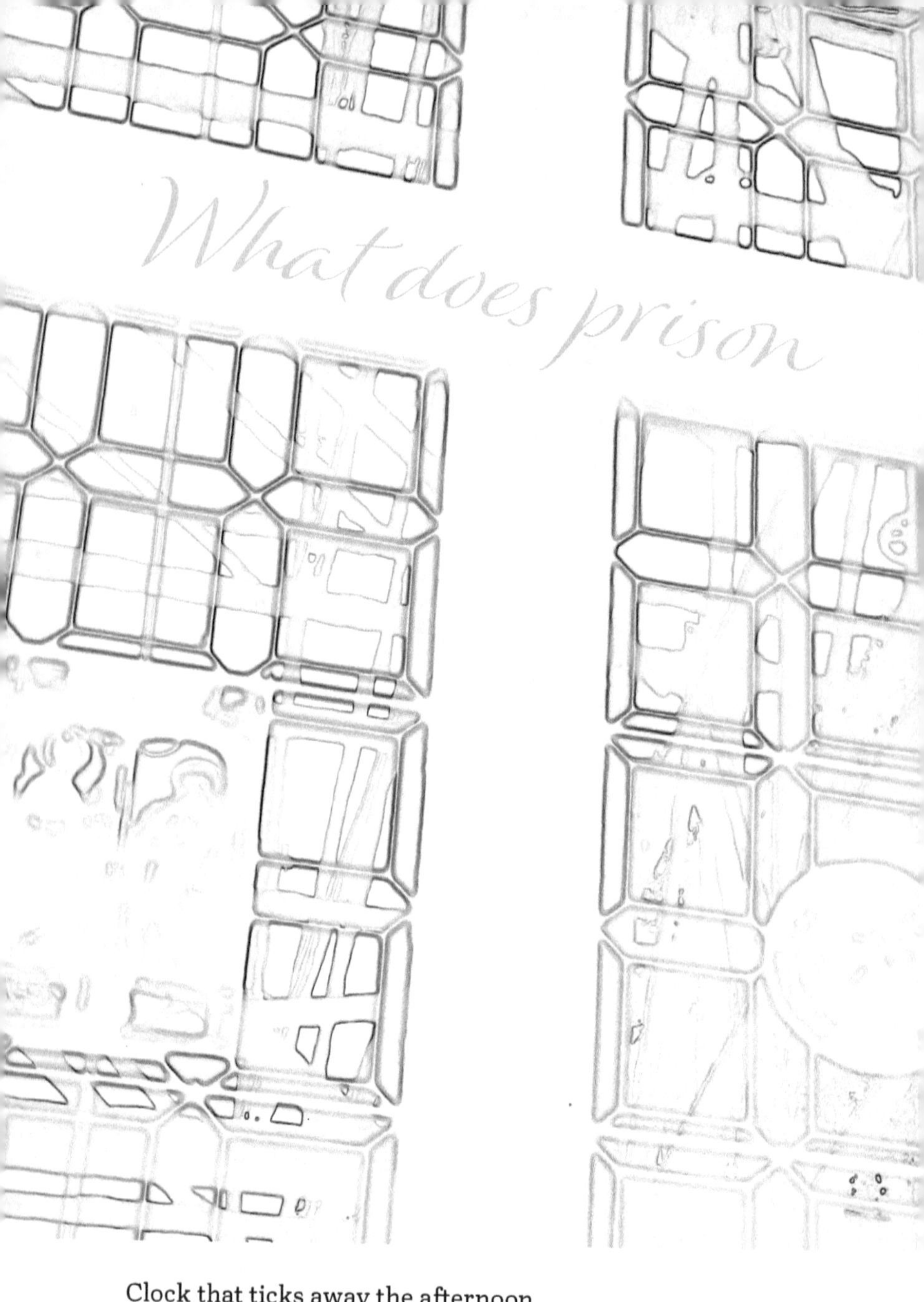

Clock that ticks away the afternoon.
Punctuates the tink of spoon on porcelain.
Choice of cream or sugar.
A slice of bread and butter.

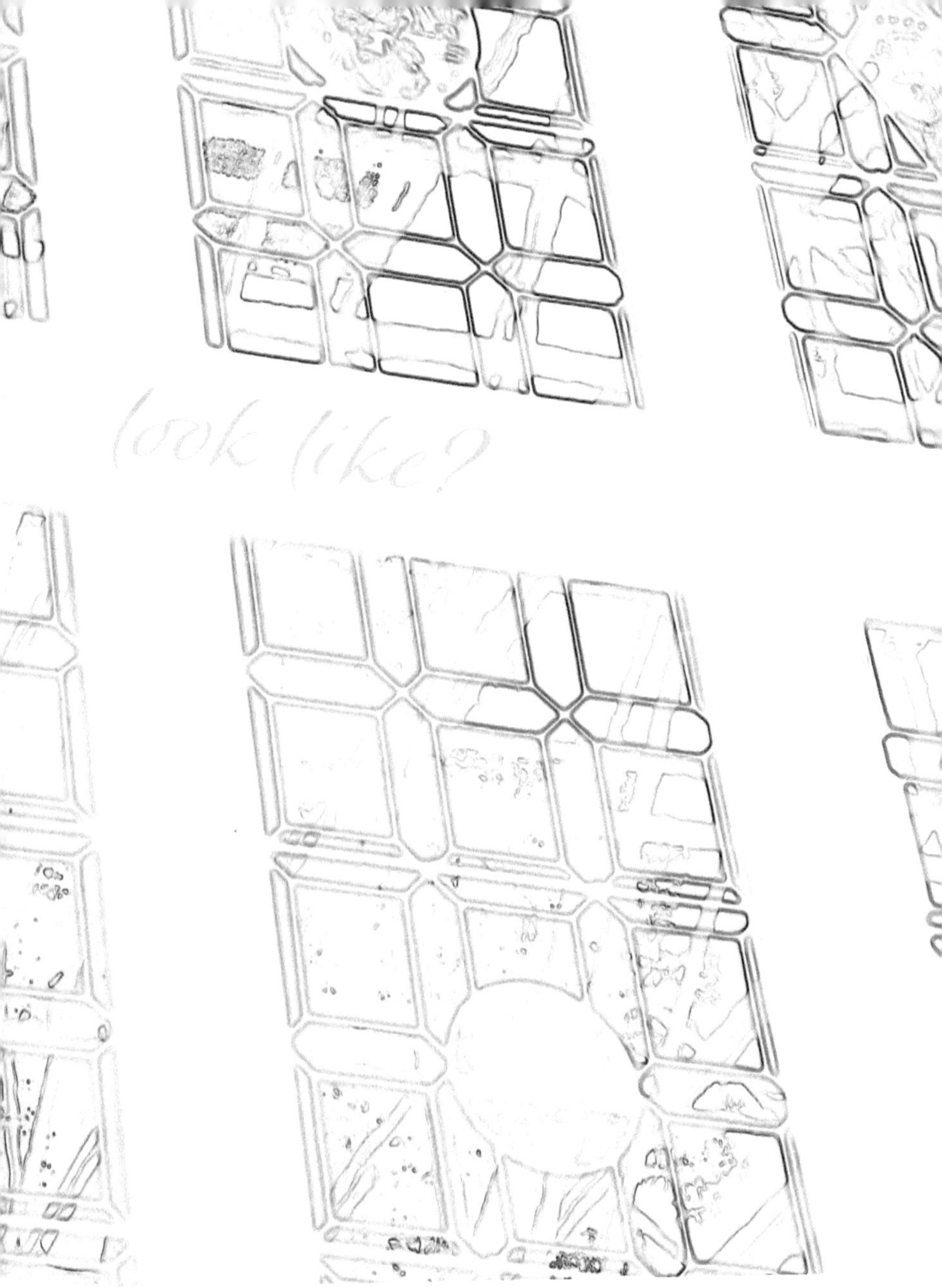

Knife-blade creases in the napkins.
Servants who hover at her elbow.
The view from tall, calm windows
across obedient lawns.

She counts the times she taps her spoon. Too many and she's being difficult, again. Too many and words are shouted, doors are slammed. Too many and she is forced to lie down. For her own good. Too many and the nurse brings a powder and a glass of water. Tink tink. Tink tink. Tink tink.

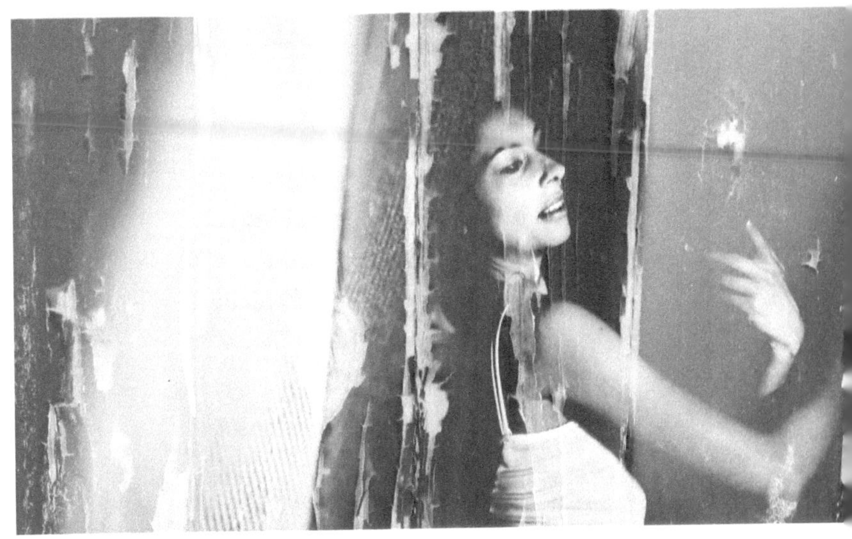

marriage?

Wives with fingers
primed with needles,
filling in the frame
with numbered colour,
following the scheme
set out for them:
a marriage with years
of tablecloths
to spread beneath
the deadweight of
roasted meats

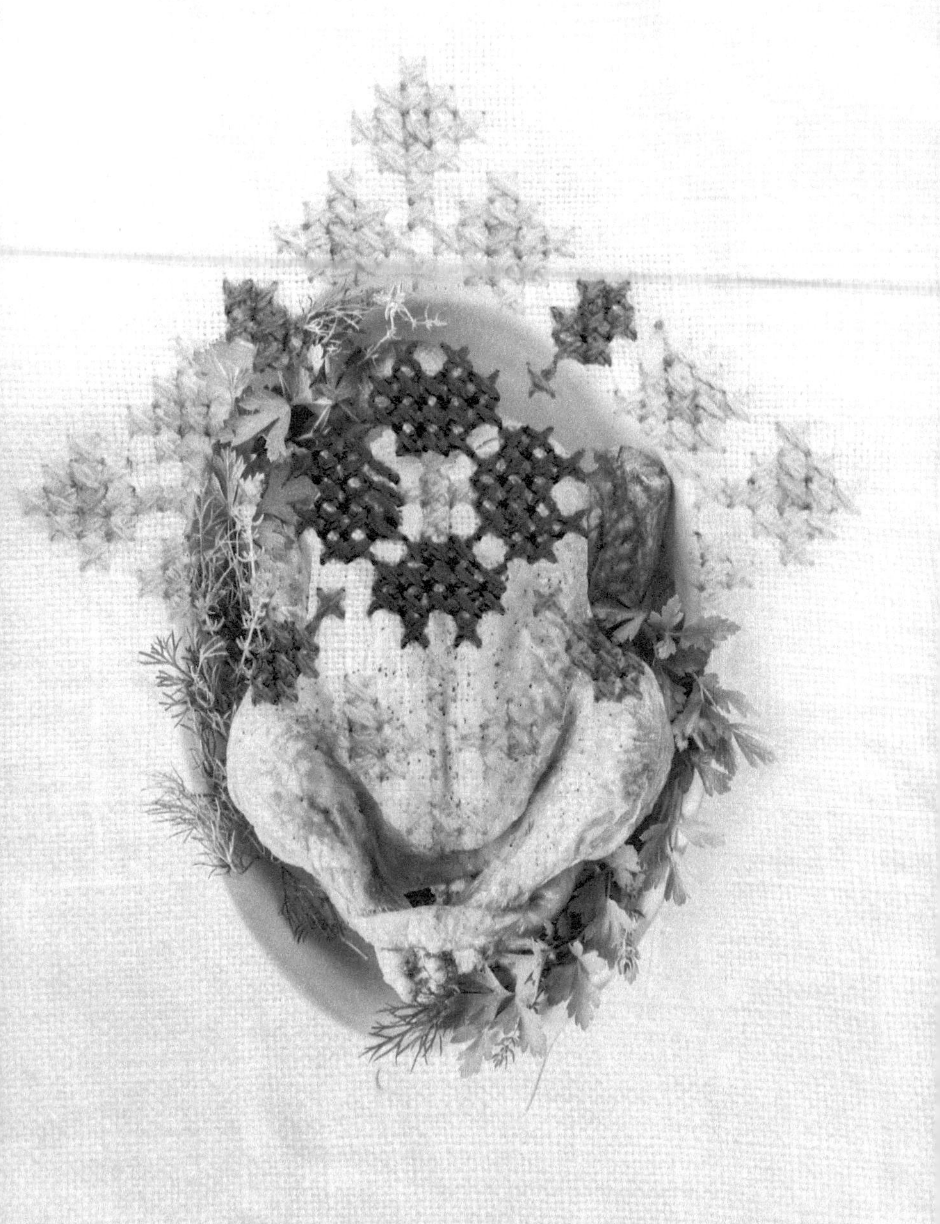

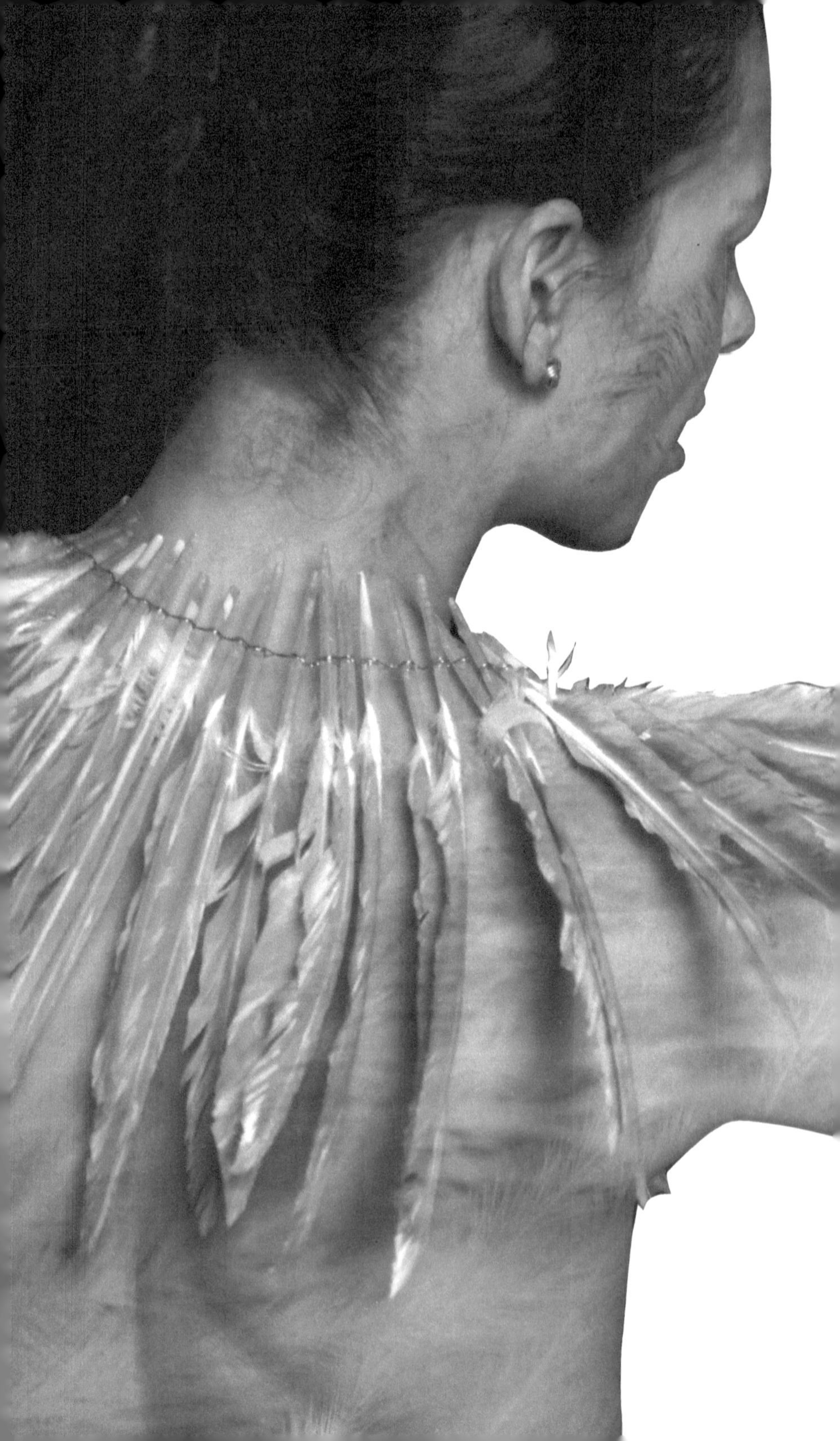

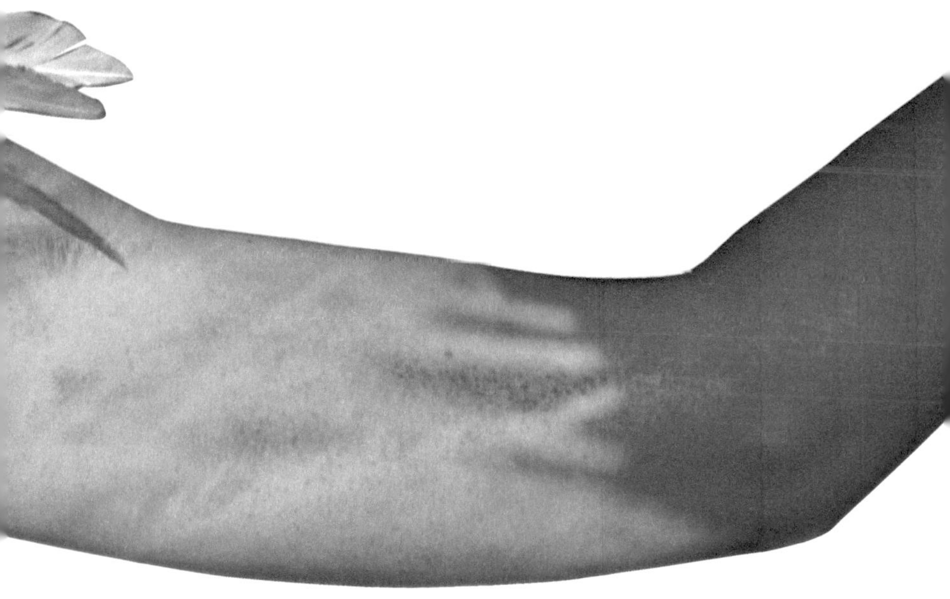

Rip out my feathers,
hang them round my throat.
They whisper round my shoulder blades,
remind me they were once wings.
Remind me how as a child I had a dream
where I took my feet off the ground and
flew.

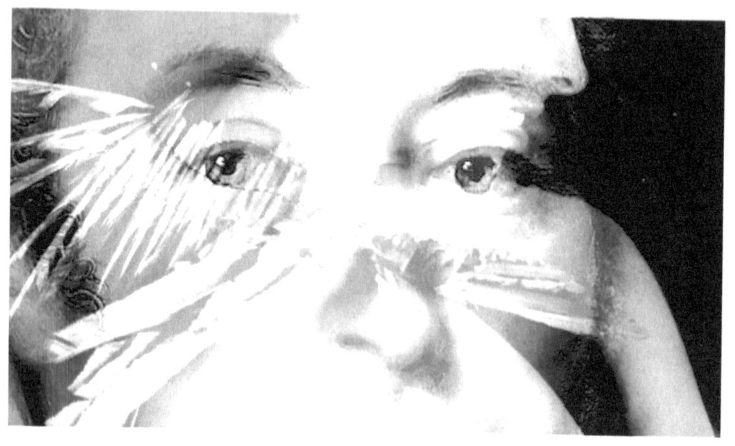

He says she needs help.
Says she needs to lie down. But
she must keep moving,
even if it's a downward spiral.

If she stops, she'll never start again.
Music box slows to a
stretched-
out
drone.

Ballerina freezes, balancing
    on one toe-tip, hands clenched
        above her head. A dancer needs music. Needs
        a hand to crank the key. Her fingers clumsy
            from lack of exercise. All they're good for
                is tapping a silver spoon against a cup.

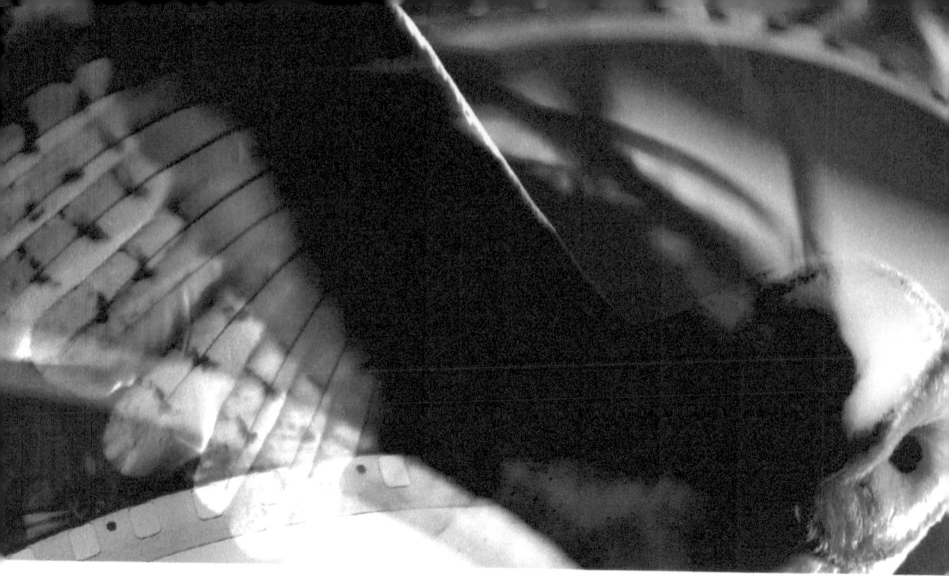

The clever ways of money. Honey versus vinegar.

He can honey, she can vinegar. With flies, he must
honey. With vinegar, she flies. Flies more. So much more.
Her wings are honey-heavy. Her angry vinegar.
His honey. Weighs her down.

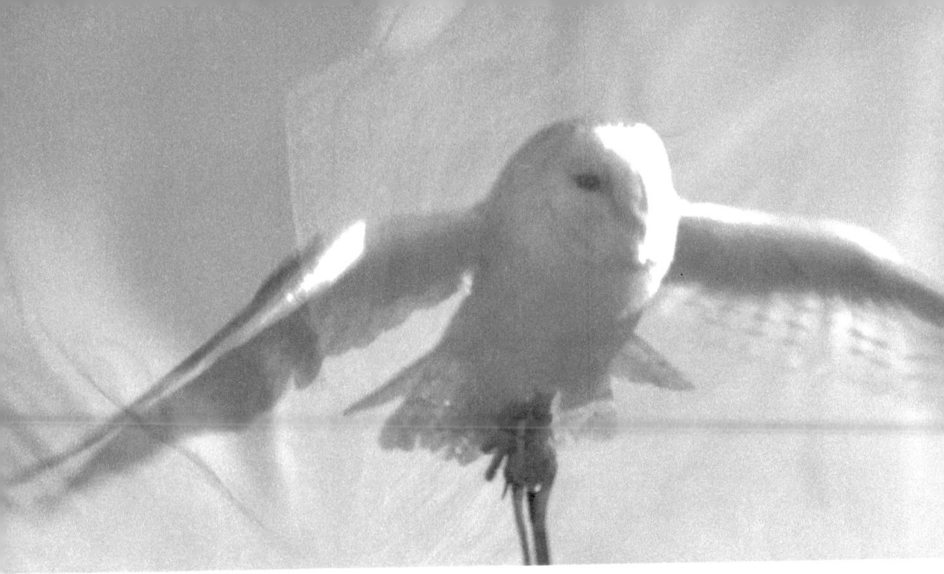

She is vinegar. Wine gone sour. She thinks vinegar wings
will save her from honey. Thinks flying will save her from
vengeance. She is a child to think the world will choose her
vinegar over his old honey. Honey always wins. One rule for
honey, another for vinegar. She doesn't see it coming. Flying
so fast, she doesn't see escape is just another solid wall.

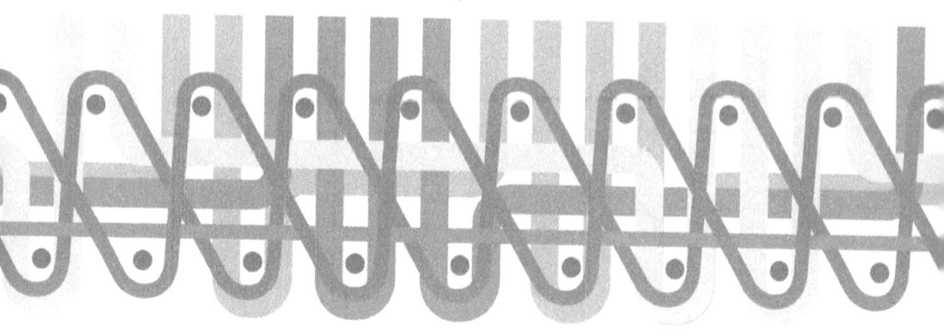

most yarn is on the surface

dimensionally stable

Look at you, he says. Running running.
How I must love you, he says, to make such a pretty gift.

She's surrounded by the proof. A crime scene scatter
of wet footprints racing away. Nowhere to run that is hers,
not even from the bath. She is possessed,
down to her bare feet. Something he can display.
In German, *gift* translates as *poison*.

little on the back

At night, she flashes knives. She slashes at the weave
but this is not embroidery to be unpicked.
Each footprint trapped, embedded, enmeshed
in the blood bone and sinew of the carpet.
Nothing can escape.

suitable for heavy wear

She hacks through to the floorboards,
leaves wounds that can't be knitted up.

designed for longevity

intricate patterns

loom interfaces face yarns

He unpeels his socks. Steps onto her woven footprints.
Treads his flesh on top of hers, stamping her flat,
squeezing his sweat into her warp and weft.

performance and design

She stamps, she paces. Hurls plates and bottles.
Storms out of arguments, slams doors. Nothing
makes the smallest dent in the carpet's armour. It shrugs off
kneeling, grovelling, begging for forgiveness.

unlimited repeat

A woman knifing at the weave. If it were embroidery
she could unpick the stitches and take them with her.
This belongs to him and always will.

and jute latex to lock
tufts in place

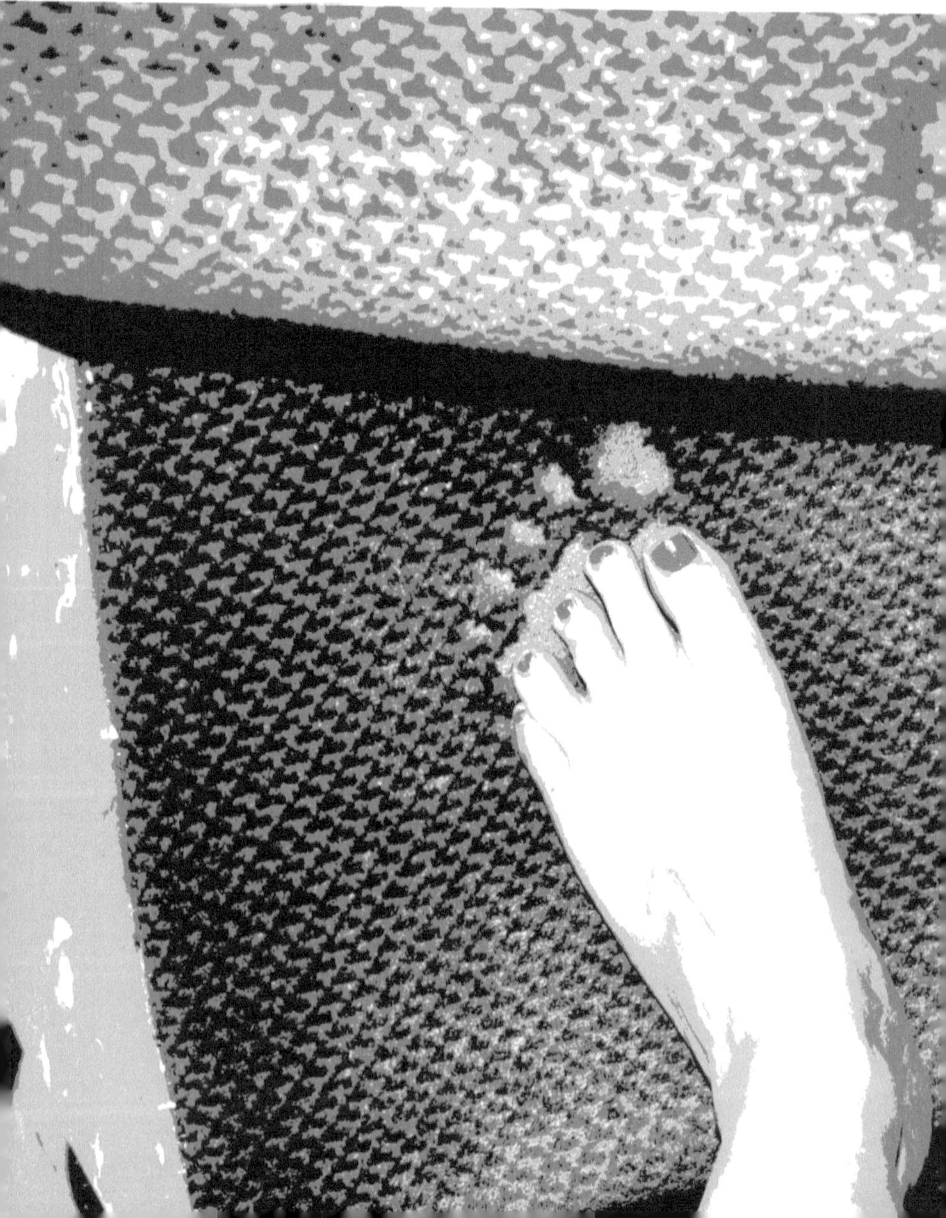
most yarn is on the surface
most yarn is on the surface

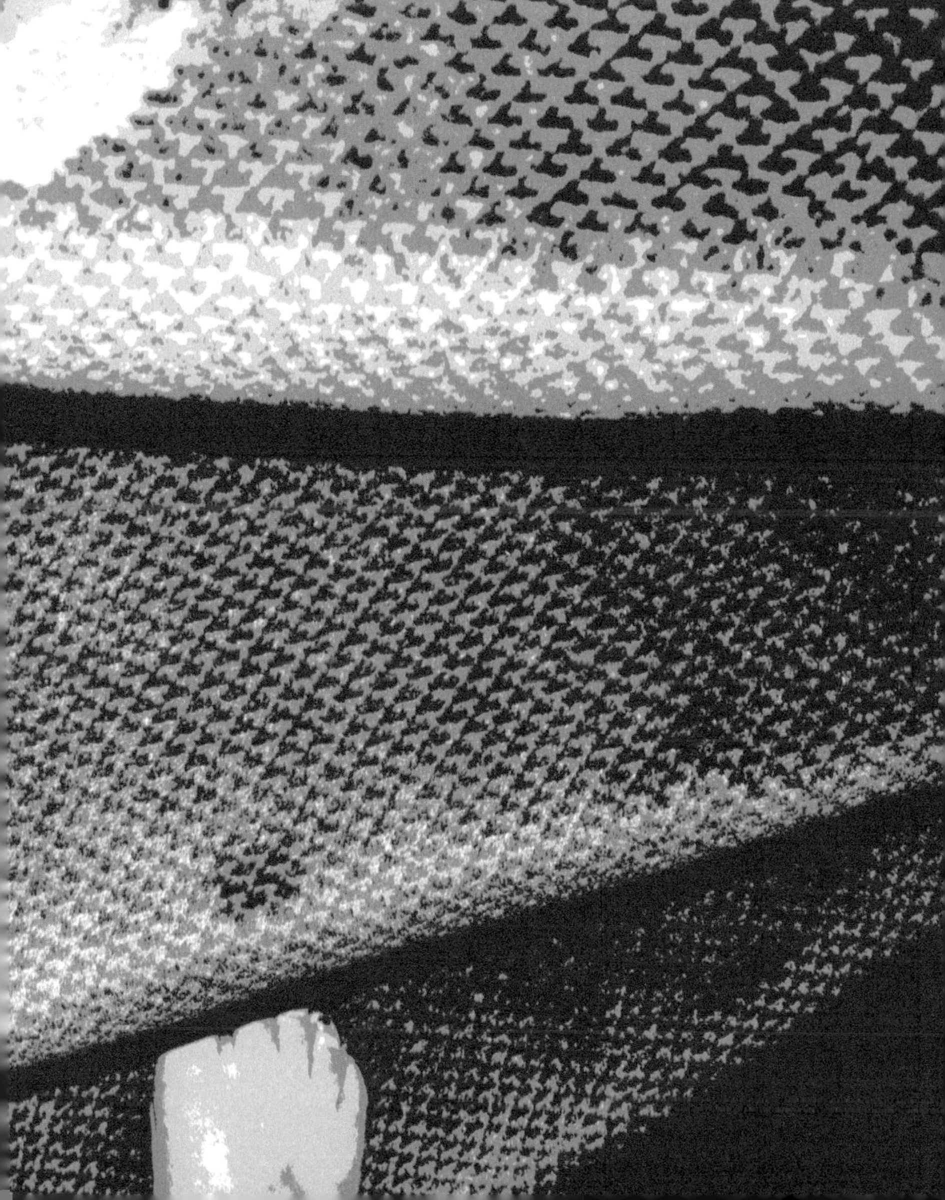

She does well, for a woman.
Has a sharp mind, for a woman.
Is muscular and lithe, for a woman.
She cannot win. Cannot be just herself.
The world's words will not permit it.

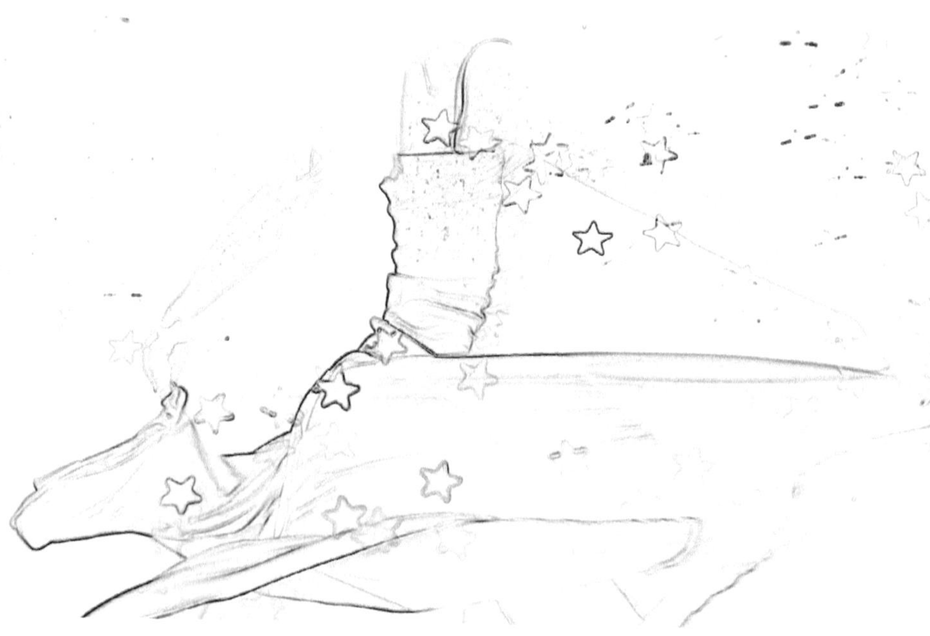

He is handsome. She is pretty.

He is firm. She is harpy.

He has goals. She has daydreams.

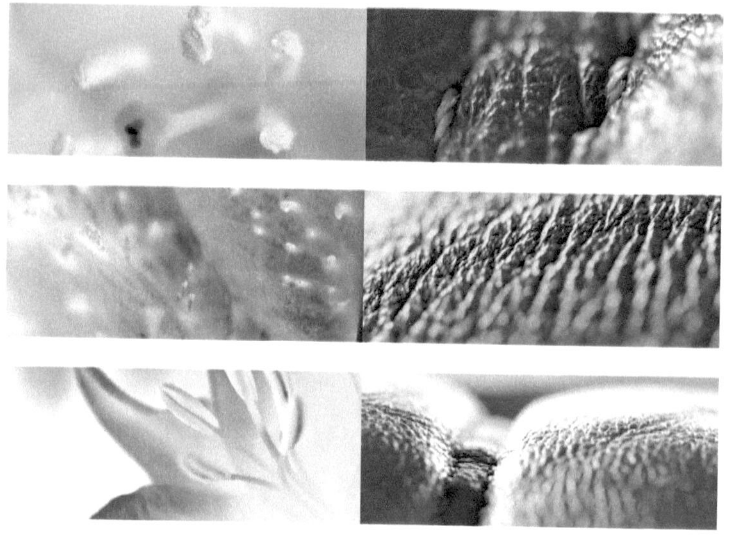

speak / gossip

stride / teeter

wild oats / slut

straight-talking / foulmouthed

faithful / clingy

diplomatic / scheming

He is talented. She is just bloody lucky.

She will never run the risk
of being taken seriously.
She is hootchie-kootchie,
belly dancer, dance-hall hoofer,
flapper, floozie, hotcha-kotcha,
black bottom bouncer, burlesque
bopper, seven-veiled Salome,
stripper exotica, go-go gal,
podium pole-swinger, lap dancer
grinder. She is a rhythm-and-boozer,
ten-cents-a-loser, up for grabs
for any man who's got a dollar bill
to stuff in her g-string.

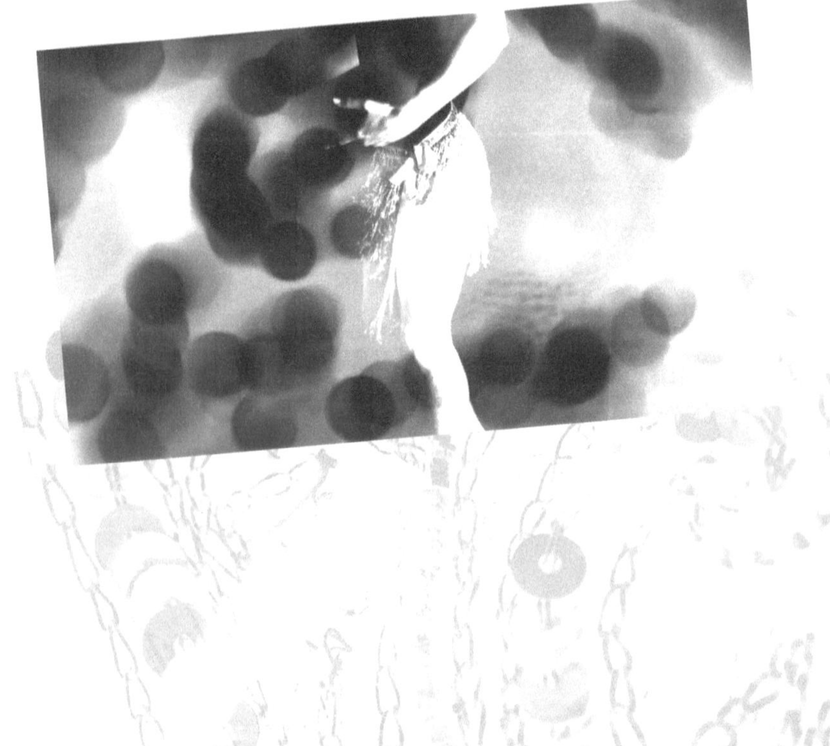

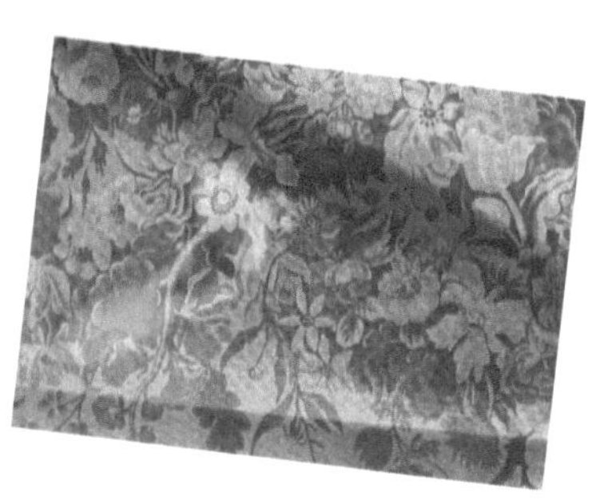

She will never run the risk
of hard landings. Will trip
on Chinese rugs, Indian rugs,
Persian rugs, Isfahan rugs,
Moroccan rugs. Cushioned as she falls
onto sofas, settees, couches,
cushions plumped that morning.

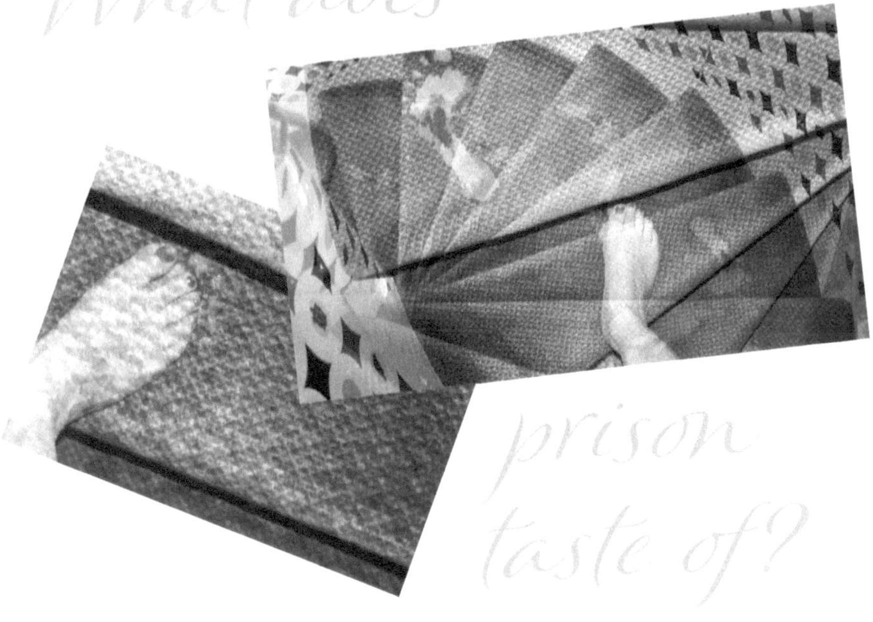

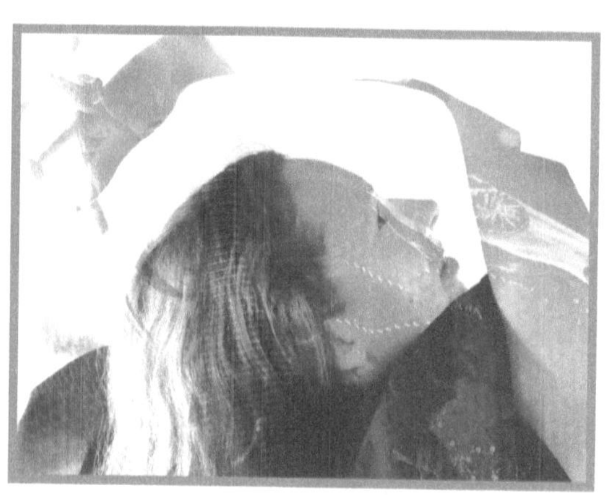

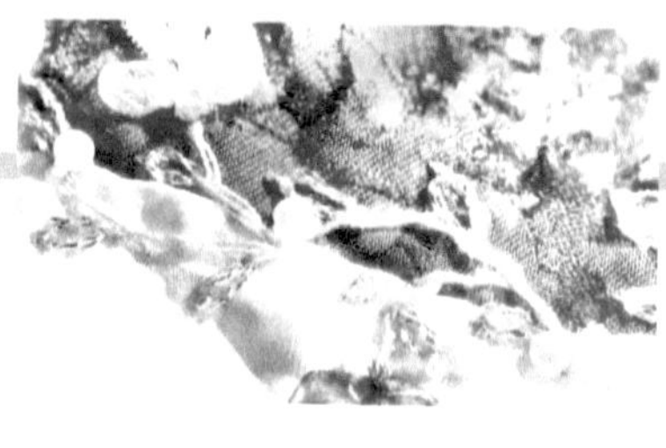

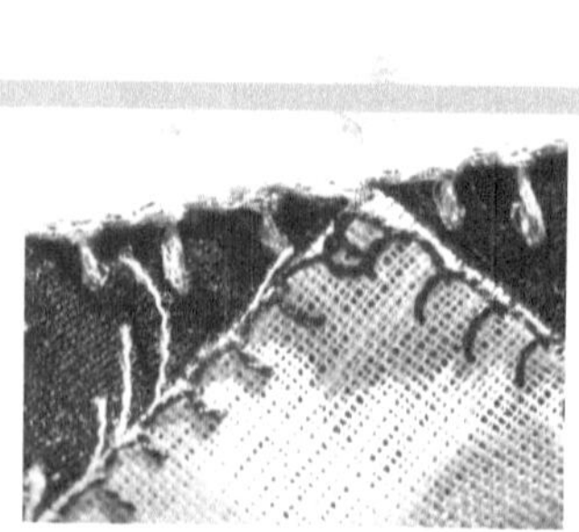

I am a multitude of swatches. A dazzle
of pattern: regency stripe and tea rose chintz,
scrap of sequin and movie star gauze;
a prince's borrowed ermine, a lover's supple suede.
I am mishmash. Work in progress.
Too many snippets to gather the wholeness
of a life. Patchwork offcuts.
A coat of clashing colours.
I am too many. I am too much.

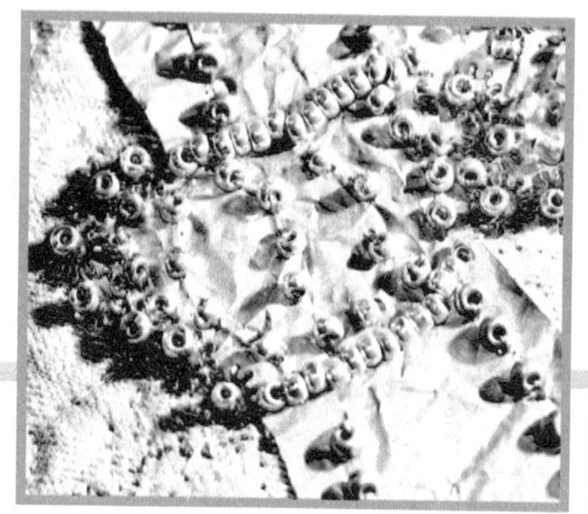

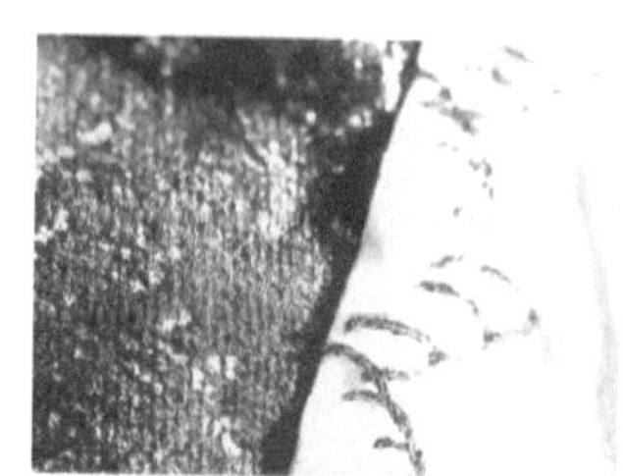

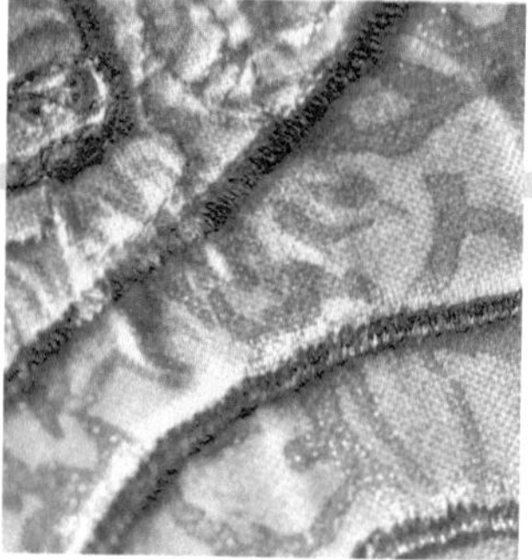

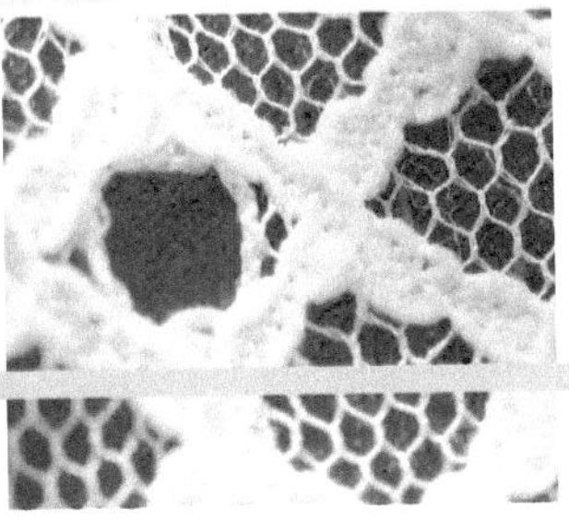

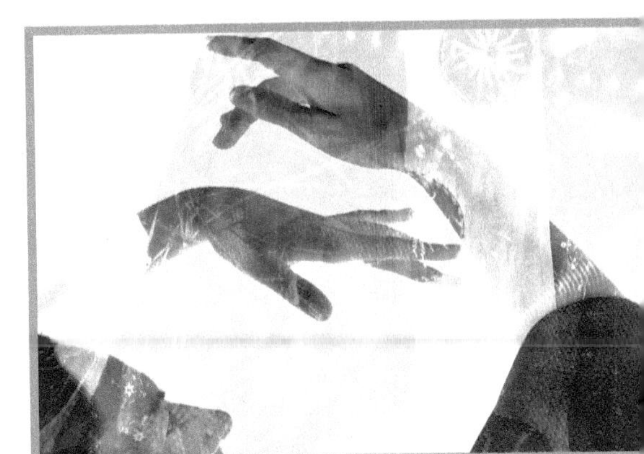

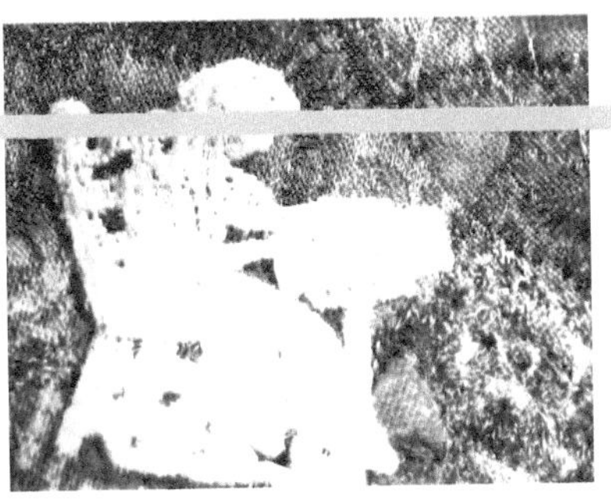

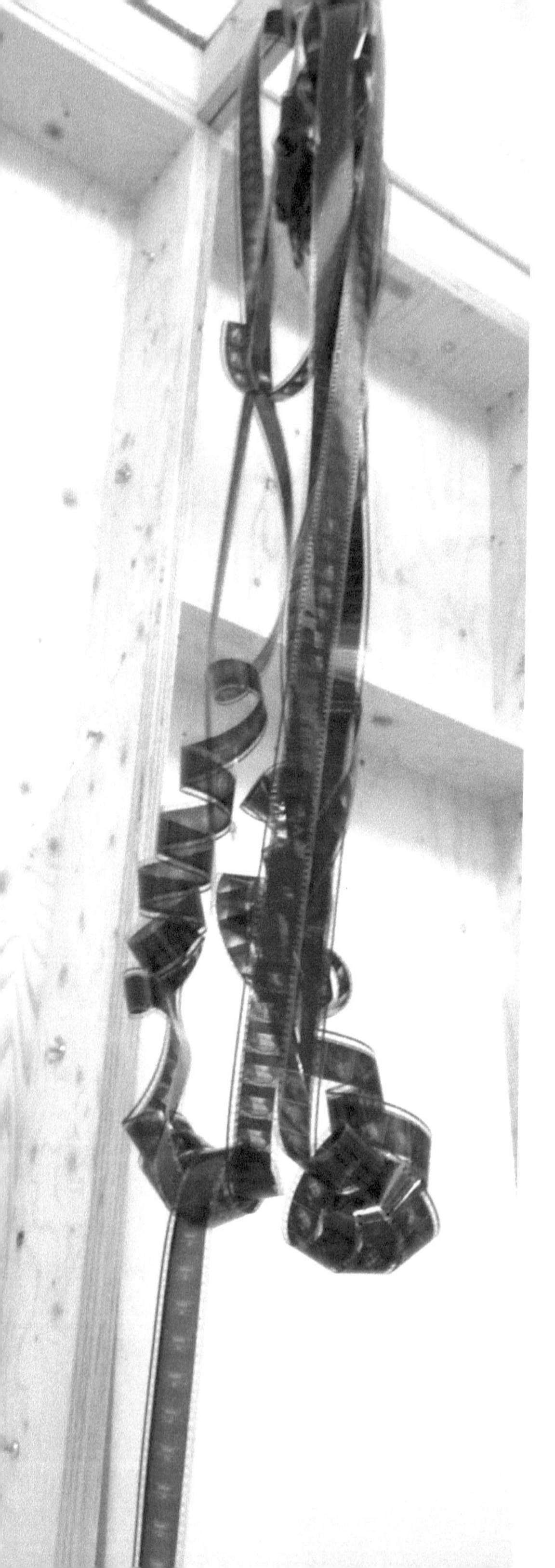

I am a collage
of film clips.
So many frames
per second. Snips
of flailing celluloid
snake across
the cutting room floor.
When I hold myself up
to the light, it looks like
dancing, flight. I am
all done with mirrors.

I am footnote. Someone's else's wife.
Little black book with half the pages missing.
Diary with months torn out. Even my name
constructed from a variety of histories.
I am never quite enough.
The truth hisses through the gaps.

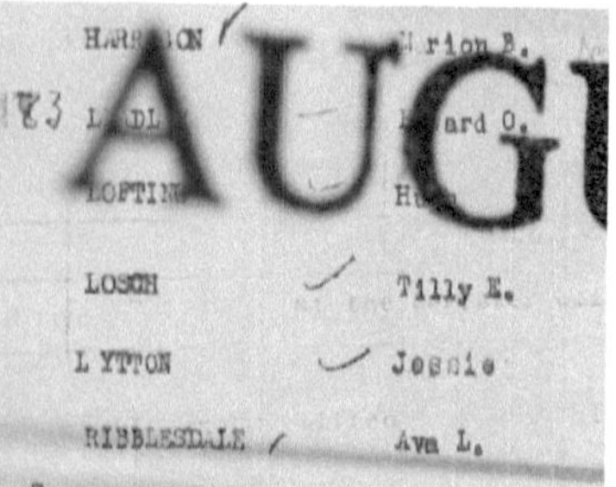

HARRISON   rion B.
S173 LAIDL   ard O.
LOFTIN   H
LOSCH   Tilly E.
LYTTON   Jessie
RIBBLESDALE   Ava L.

EGRAMS ENQUIRY" or call with this f
nied by this form, and, if possible, the env

petition

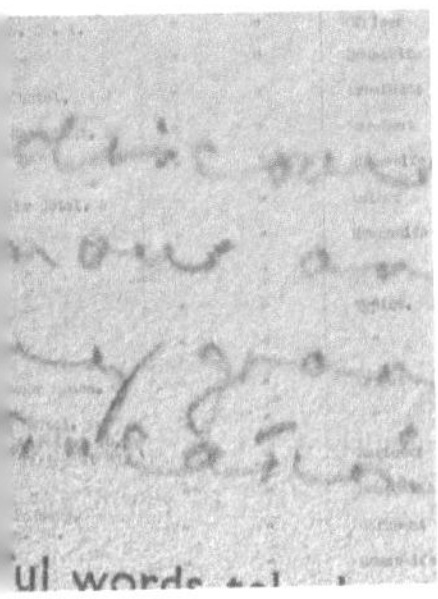

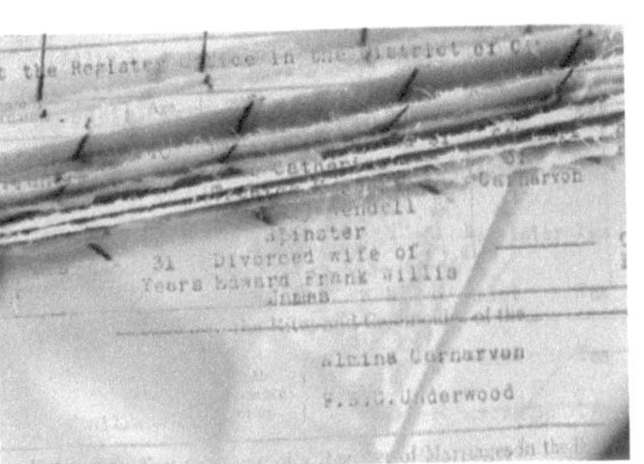

t the Register Office in the District of Ca...

Carnarvon ... of Carnarvon

...endell
Spinster
31   Divorced wife of
Years Edward Frank Willis
James

...almina Carnarvon

...F.S.C. Underwood

...of Marriages in the...

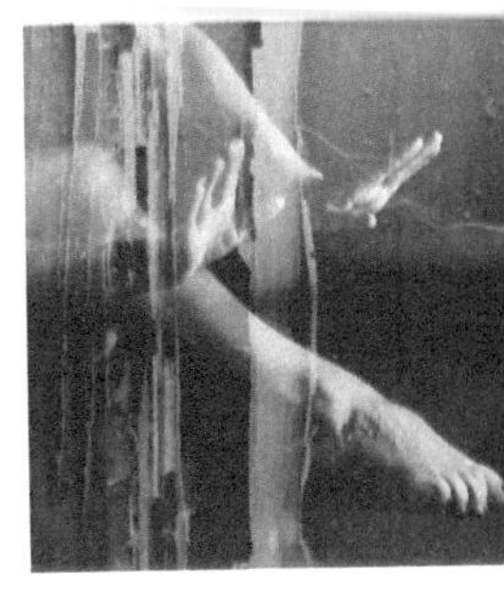

Night is the only room
to which she owns the key.
In her dreams she flies,
and does not fall. Wild
and incandescent with her truth.
Her crowds applaud, adore, approve.
Brava, encora. They understand.
They feed her night-time half.

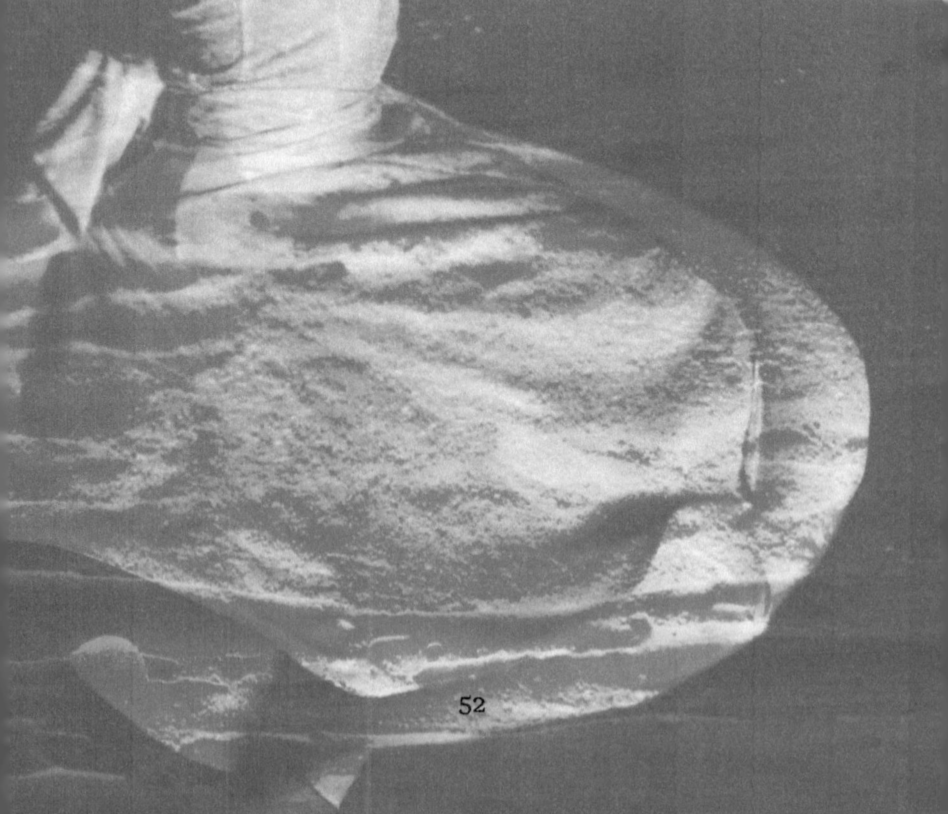

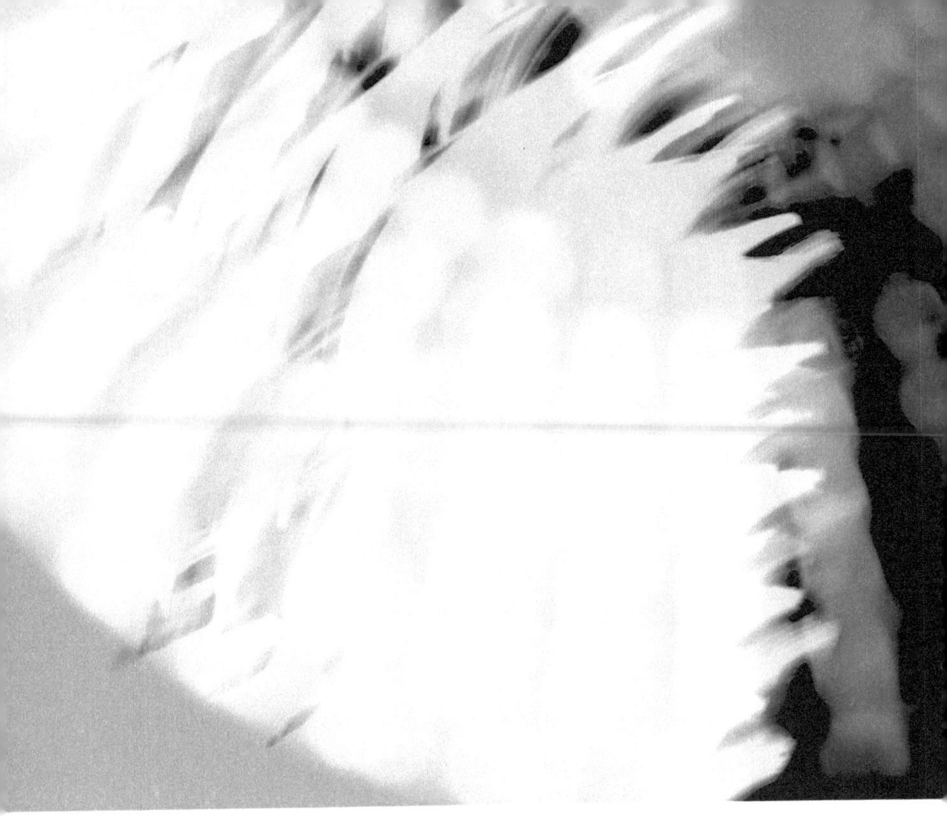

She grows unbalanced. Half-gorged,
half-starved. Gravity skews. Axis tilts.
She totters in dizzy circles round
a tipped core. Faster and faster,
further and further from the true. She loses
compass bearings, till north is south.
She doesn't know which way is up.
What to believe. Or who.

I was never one for words. I could not
read the warning signs. The small
print. The scandal sheets. Sticks and
stones. Names can never.

My hands are the opposite of
clutching. They know the truth
of letting go. The truth
of what I cannot hold onto.
Fingers smooth from all the money
that's passed through.

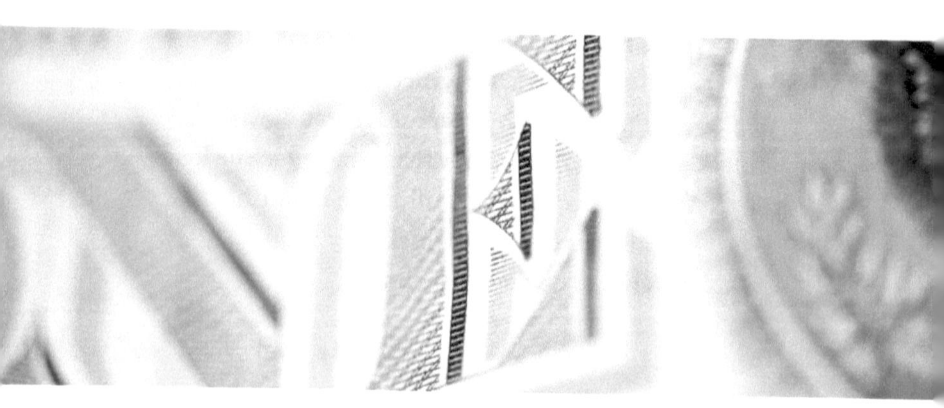

I am another beloved rarity,
hung alongside the Dalis, the Ernsts,
the Magrittes. A bequeathed Canopic jar.
All those collectibles. I am the only one
that insists on breathing.

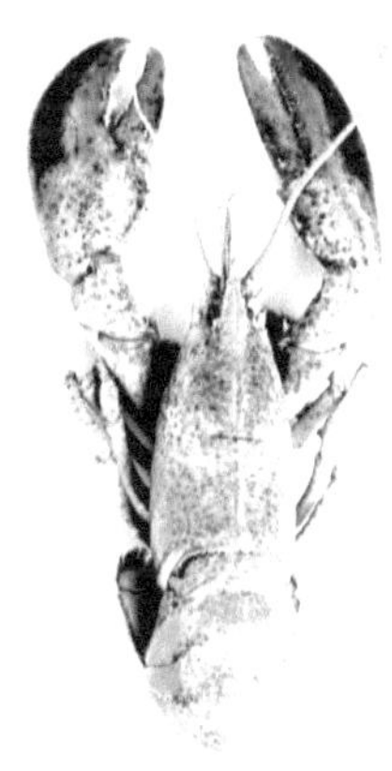

She ribbons up her ballet pumps. Dances
where and when no-one can see. Dances
for herself, in a dervish spin, faster
and closer to a deity she can't believe in.
Spits in the eye of little gods and husbands
as she slingshots past their sun, picking up speed.

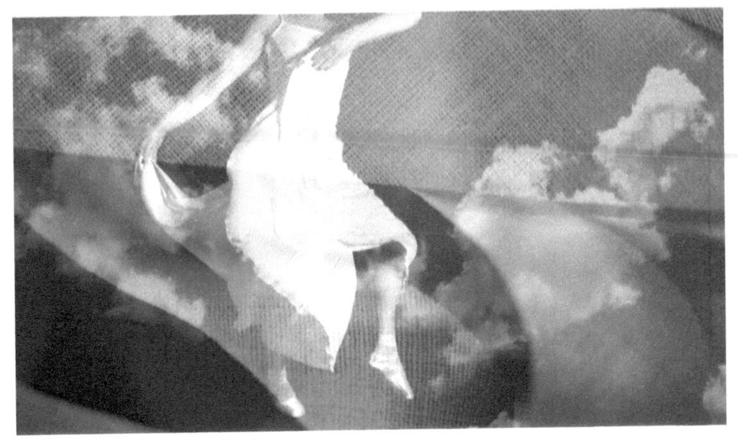

What will I
          find there?

Here she is again, flinging her comet
away from a star she'll come back to
this year next year sometime whenever.
All comets fly in closed orbits, however bright
fast clever wild they think themselves.

They're locked in, can't escape.
The only escape is to dance
and keep dancing, till they plunge into the fire.

I am electric. I am on fire,
my bones and body burn.
A moving target. Never
one place long enough
for evidence to stack up.
Fingerprints melt from cocktail glasses,
lipstick slides from collars,
kisses evaporate on lovers' lips.
My eyes are blue. No, hazel.
No, green with copper flecks.

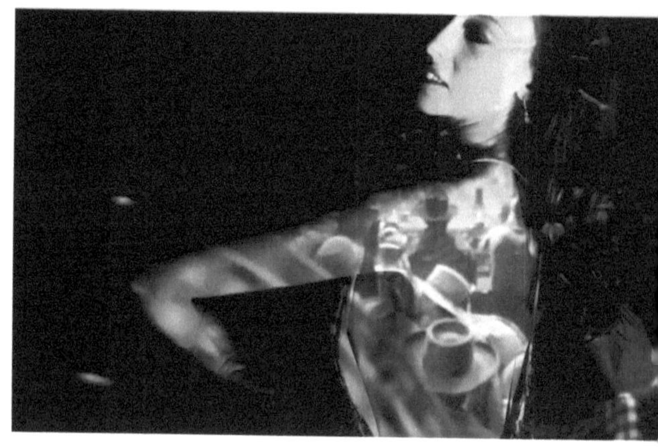

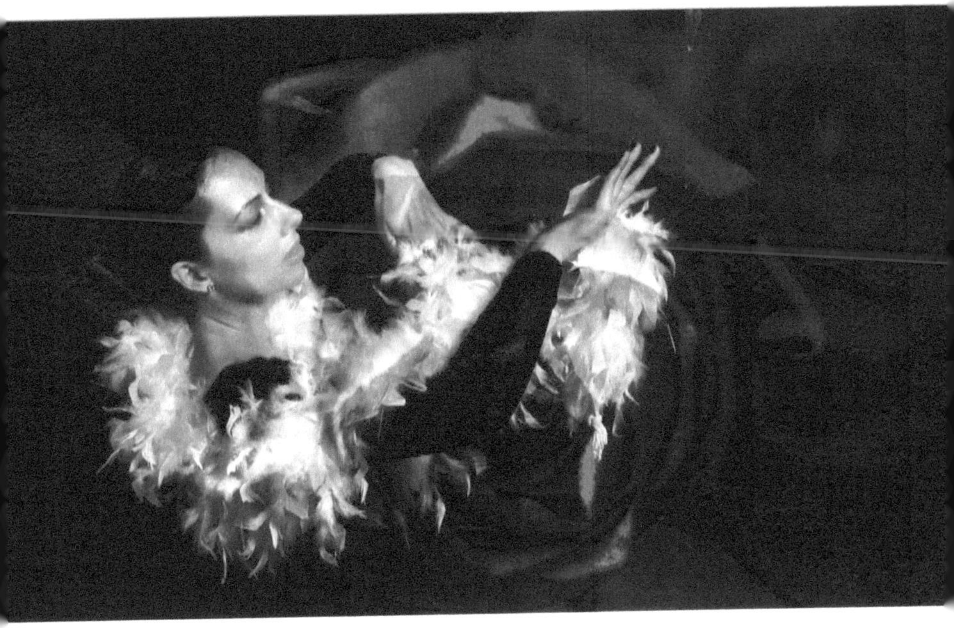

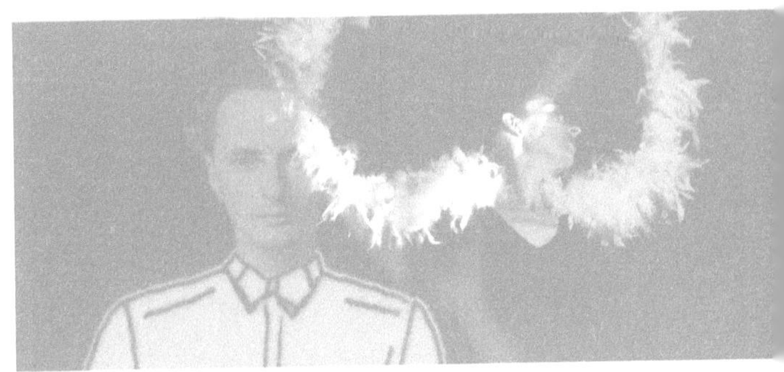

She danced off the page, off the end of the dotted line.
Shrugged away the planet's atmosphere.

Seeking out a universe where this
is not the story. A universe where
she can write her own.

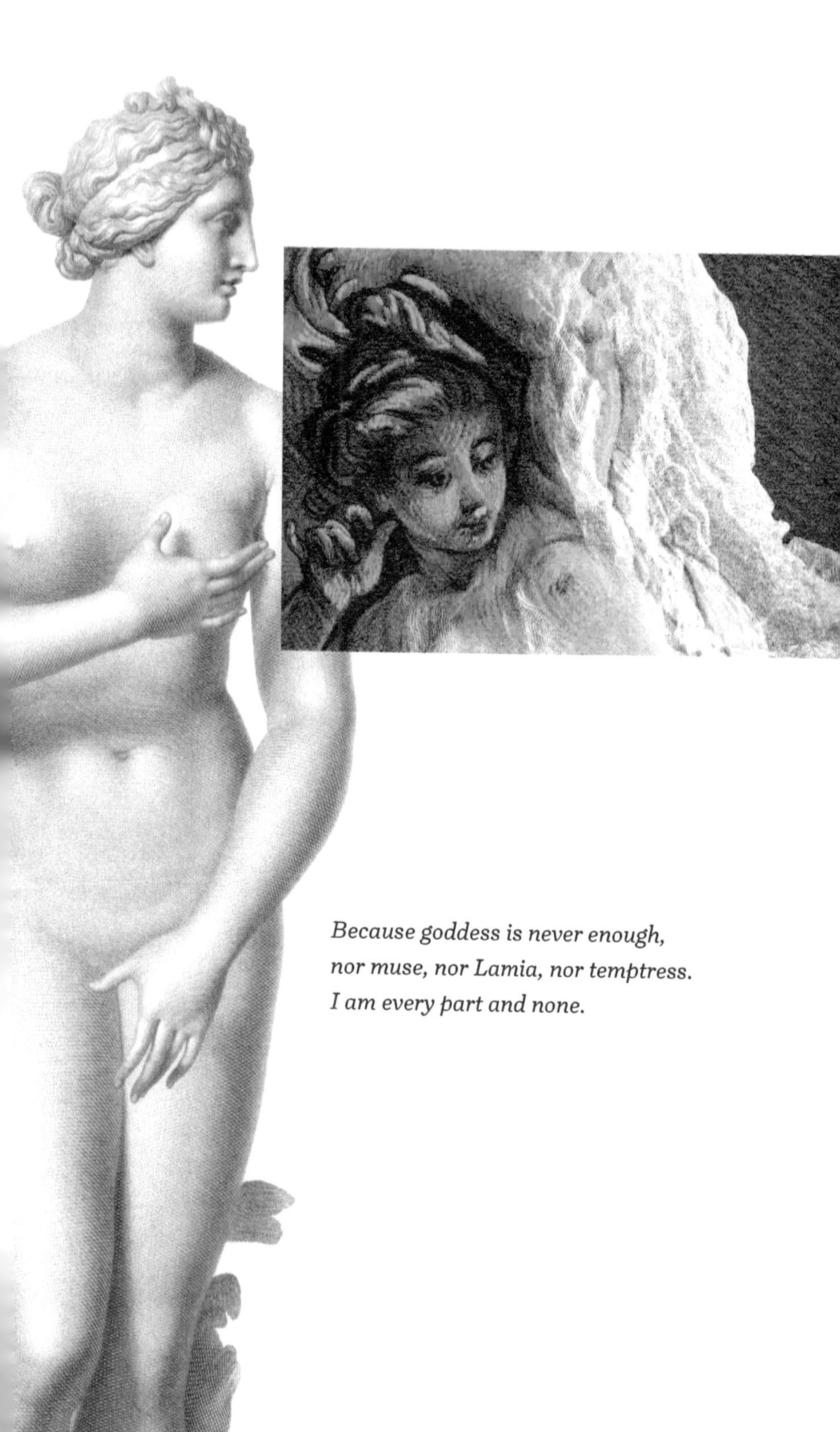

Because goddess is never enough,
nor muse, nor Lamia, nor temptress.
I am every part and none.

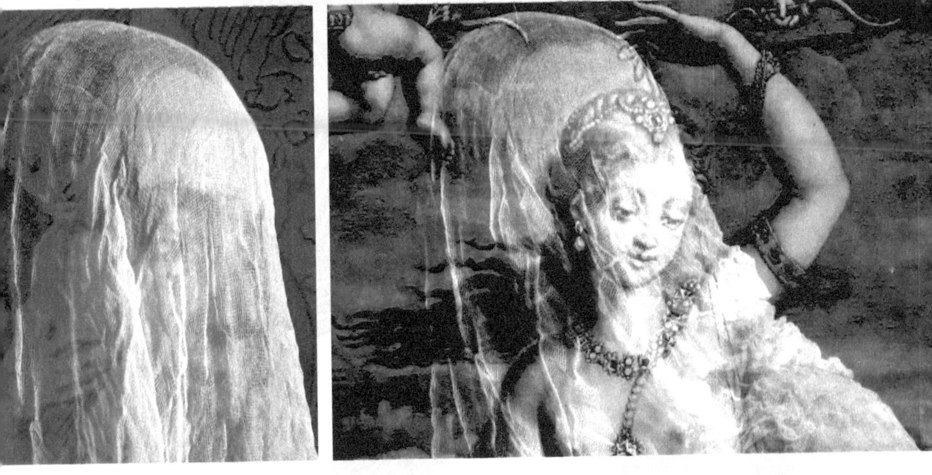

*Nothing about me is a lie, and nothing
true. I elude definitions, marriages,
friends and enemies, health and sickness,
death do her part.*

Because I cannot be pinned, stitched,
hemmed, woven, weft or warped.

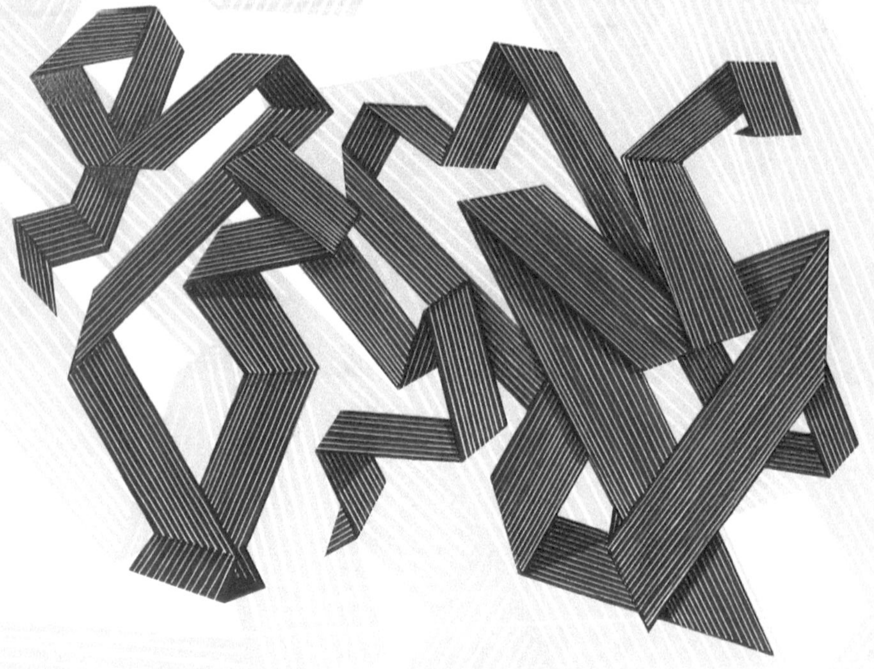

Because cat's cradle, because hopscotch,
ring-a-roses, because all fall down.
Because I fall between
other people's lives. And falling is flying,
if you turn it on its side and look at it the other way.

Because I am higher than the sky.
Because I am the dance and not the dancer,
the flight and not the wing,
the shimmer not the star.
I am water round a rock,
storm that rages through the trees,
lightning that floods the night,
thunder that hammers down the sky,
the houses beneath it, castles, tents and little men.

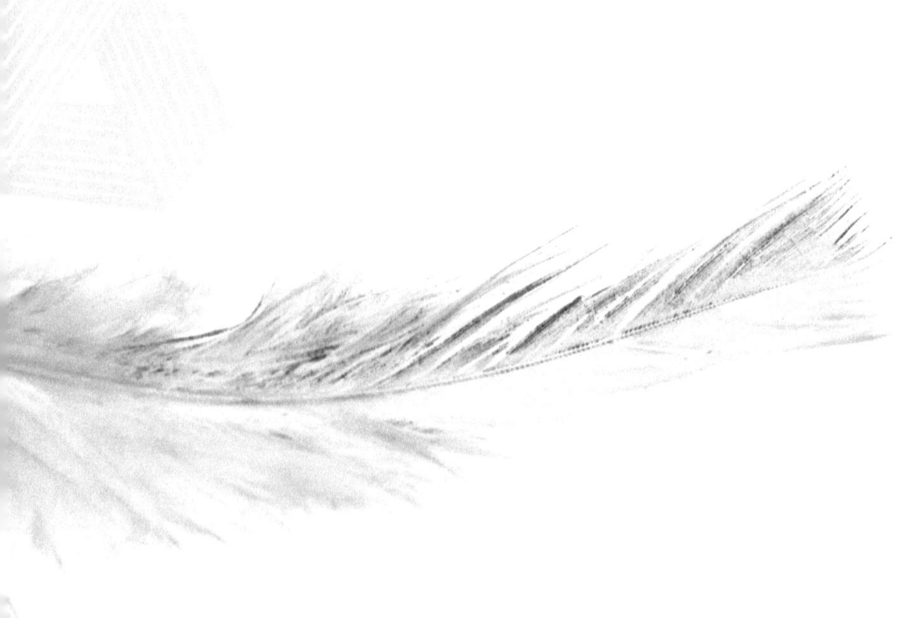

With best wishes

I am the one who gets away.

This book began as poetry film. I became fascinated by the life of Tilly and where she would keep popping up ... at West Dean College (the one time home of her first husband Edward James) and the spiral footprint carpet, at a Royal Academy exhibition in the work of Joseph Cornell, at Highclere Castle, and in the lives of so many famous men. Eventually I couldn't resist ... my interpretation of her story needed to be told.

I would like to thank Rosie Garland for being so up for a dive into the world of Tilly, for her wonderful writing, performance and for being so encouraging and supportive throughout the process of making the film and this book.

For embodying Tilly so beautifully I thank my dancer and model Natasha Jervis. And for her wonderful voice, I thank Alison Glennie – a beautiful thing rose from some dark days.

I've had brilliant support from my mentor Rosalind Davis: who helped to kickstart me; keep me going; get funding; and get it out there.

Tilly's biographer William Cross has been incredibly generous with sharing his contacts and research material.

For other help and support along the way I thank:
Amelia Britton, Sarah Brown, Lucy English, Fresh Shoot Studios, Nina Hoggarth, Fintan McKahey, Jim Snowden, Mat Thorpe, Andrew Wheeler, Lucie Wilson.

Jane Glennie

All images created by Jane Glennie.
Some are originals for this book, some are stills
from the film *Because Goddess is Never Enough*

Page 6: Genthe photograph collection, Library
of Congress, Prints and Photographs Division.
Page 63: goddess from the Rijksmuseum,
Amsterdam. Page 63/64: incorporates an
original painting by Sarah Brown, inspired by
Tilly Losch, Les Ballets 1933 and The Seven
Deadly Sins.

The film 'Because Goddess is Never Enough'
was supported by Arts Council England.

To watch the film please see
www.janeglennie.co.uk

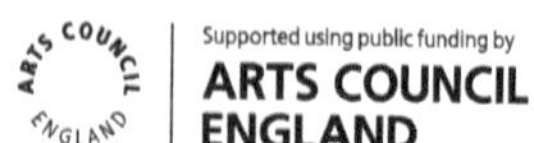